# FIND
# YOUR
# PASSION

*A story by*

## ARNIE WARREN

Pall
Fort Lau

Published by:

Pallium Books

7027 West Broward Boulevard # 272

Fort Lauderdale, Florida 33317 U.S.A.

arniewarren@msn.com • www.greatconnection.com

Library of Congress Catalog Card Number: 99-97827

ISBN 0-9655148-7-0

Printed in the United States of America

10  9  8  7  6  5  4  3  2  1

*Dedicated to those who
always knew there was
something they were
put on earth to do
but didn't know
how to find it.*

# ACKNOWLEDGMENTS

I WOULD LIKE TO THANK Carolyn Kerner Stein who introduced me to Malaysia; Rameez Yahaya at the Malaysian Consulate and Yuslen of the Embassy of Malaysia; Steve Behar, Behar Shirt Company, who shared his company's history and instructed me in the shirt manufacturing process; Don Donaldson, Barton & Donaldson Shirtmakers in Philadelphia, whose technical advice was invaluable; Kathleen Field for her constant support and Katherine Glover, INTI Publishing, for her suggestions.

Joyce Abbott, Ph.D., Rita Ackrill, Jim Barber, Stephen Baberadt, Julia Connor, Joan McGrane Cutlip, Richard Fuller, Joy Krause, Caroline Mansur, Marlene Naylor, Theresa Nelson, Sal and Judy Ronci, Anne Stanton, Angie Tennyson, Julie Thompson, Mary Westheimer, and Ron White. Thank you all for your suggestions during the completion of this book.

Finally, Linda Sacha—editor, friend and mentor. I've come to know that her contribution is not for me alone. Linda sees the big picture and, in this case, gave freely of her special gifts that you might find your place in life that much sooner.

# APPRECIATION

I WOULD LIKE TO EXPRESS MY GRATITUDE to Edith Donohue, Ph.D. for her generosity in allowing usage of the concepts set forth in this book.

Dr. Donohue, a graduate of Johns Hopkins University, maintains a counseling practice to help clients find the career they are suited for. Her process involves a 90-minute interview that delves into their past to reveal their special gifts. Her research in this area became the focal point of her doctoral thesis at Union Institute Graduate School.

Dr. Donohue's gift is the ability to probe and listen, then translate the mosaic of recollections and thoughts she hears into something tangible the client can apply. As Dr. Donohue says, "Finding one's gift is the cornerstone of a fulfilling career—a career that uses that gift in paid work and service to others. Acting on your basic gift, then, is always what brings satisfaction and joy in life."

While this story is fictional, the basic concepts are sound—rooted in well-researched fact that has helped hundreds find their niche in life. We hope you find our efforts beneficial.

E.D./A.W.

*"Passion is a key ingredient in building
a successful pattern in life. It is the source
of inspiration and creativity. It builds inner
determination, hopes, and aspirations.
Without passion, it is difficult to establish realistic
goals and to develop plans to achieve those goals."**

— James W. McLamore

*James W. McLamore, The Burger King, ©1998, McGraw-Hill.
Re-produced with permission of the McGraw-Hill Companies.

# FIND

# YOUR

# PASSION

# FOREWORD

**O**NCE THERE WAS A TIME when men and women had no choice in their life's occupation. You were born to follow the trade of your father or to lead an unfulfilled life of royal privilege. So the question, *"What am I passionate about doing in life?"* rarely passed the lips of the average man or woman—for thousands of years.

Today, everyone has the freedom to ask that question. But sadly, many can't find the answer because they have never been told *how.*

In this story you will read about a young man named Zaine as he learns and applies three simple steps to the career he was meant to have—three simple steps that will show you how to FIND *YOUR* PASSION.

# ONE

*11PM—THE NIGHT YOU PROPOSED TO ME.*

*My dearest Zaine,*

*I told you I'd give you my decision in the morning, but I know if I faced you I wouldn't be able to say what is in my heart without bursting into tears. I would weaken and fall into your arms before I could even begin. So, it is with a full heart that I'm writing my thoughts to you.*

*Please know that these words are written because I care for you—for us—so deeply.*

*Zaine, I want you to look with me to your future. Your father has built his shirt factory here in Malaysia, and he is turning more responsibility over to you. I am not belittling the importance of your work. I simply wonder if this is what you want to do for the rest of your life. I don't see any passion for it in your eyes. Zaine, you cannot live—really live—without a passion for your work. Because you're an American, I thought you could do whatever you wanted to do in life. Where did that spirit go? My love, look around, look beyond our town of Batupura, find what you'd love to do most in life and bring that passion back to me.*

*Because I love you so much, I want to say 'yes' to your proposal, but . . . please, for now, take this time to focus on just you—for our happiness. Does that make sense? I pray you'll find it in a reasonable time.*

*I'm off to Hong Kong. The management institute has hired me to consult on an educational program they are putting together.*

*My dear, this may be the hardest letter you'll ever read or that I have ever written, but I send it to you with tenderness and love.*

*Forever yours,*

*Rayna*

Zaine let the letter drop into his lap as he sat on the porch steps of his cottage and gazed out at the mountains of Batupura, diffused in a purple haze. His chest tightened. The woman he admired and adored and whom he wanted for his wife had sent a shock wave through him.

The thought of losing Rayna was devastating, and the thought—the nagging thought—of never knowing what he wanted to be when he grew up loomed again like a recurring demon in his mind. It had gnawed away at him through his childhood, his teen years, to now. And Rayna had validated this lack.

He looked over toward his father's home and could see the older man walking on the veranda. When Atan saw him, he stopped and motioned his son to come over.

Zaine did not want to move. He was numb with shock but pushed himself up and, clutching the letter in his hand, walked along the path to his father's house.

## TWO

"GOOD MORNING, SON," SAID ATAN.

Zaine did not respond as he climbed the step to the veranda.

"Are you all right?"

He thrust the letter into his father's hands. Atan searched his son's eyes as he accepted the letter and moved toward a white wicker chair on the veranda. As Atan sat, he fingered his glasses from his shirt pocket, put them on and read Rayna's letter.

Zaine sat in the chair opposite his father, arms tightly folded over his stomach. He gazed along the gray veranda, beyond his father, past the randomly placed urns, thick with ferns, to the corner of the house where a blue and yellow hammock hung limply in the morning stillness.

19

His father looked up from the letter. "Ah, Zaine," he sighed, and he stood up and went behind his son's chair. He put a firm grip on Zaine's shoulder, then a massaging motion as he leaned close and whispered, "You have found a good woman, son. A very good woman," he added soothingly.

"A good woman breaks your heart?" said Zaine, his voice rough with emotion, his face drained and expressionless.

"This is a woman whose love is so deep she risks losing you so you can find yourself," Atan said nodding his head several times to affirm his words as he returned to his chair.

Zaine stood up and walked to the edge of the veranda, his back to his father. "Why did she do this to me?"

"She didn't do it *to* you, she did it *for* you," said Atan.

Again they were silent.

"I think I'll go to Hong Kong and talk with her."

"And what would you say when you got there?"

"I don't know. I'm so confused. I'm upset and angry—hurt angry. Yet somehow I love her even more."

Atan looked off to the distant mountains as he gathered his thoughts. "I find myself agreeing with Rayna's wisdom. What's missing in your life is the opportunity to explore and discover what *you'd* like to do."

"I thought I was doing what I was supposed to."

Atan raised an eyebrow, and Zaine suddenly realized he was doing what his *father* wanted him to do and had given up on the thought of trying to discover what *he* wanted to do. And *that* is what Rayna wanted him to think about. "I'm happy doing what I'm doing," he said defensively.

"Really," said Atan sardonically. "Then where's the passion that Rayna speaks of?"

"Are you on her side?"

"We are both on your side, son. You love Rayna?"

"Of course."

"She wants you to love your work as passionately as you love her."

"But I don't know what my passion is! Dad, we've been through this a hundred times. You and Mom always asked me what I wanted to do. I still don't know. I don't even know how to begin!"

"She told you in her letter."

"She asked me to look around."

"Well, look around then," said his father.

"Look around for *what*?" he snapped.

"For what you'd most like to do in life."

"And by looking around, I'll somehow magically discover it?"

Atan leaned back straining the wicker. "If you want Rayna you must leave here. You can't *hope* you'll find it, you have to take *action* to find it."

Zaine searched for some softness in his father's look but could see only a stolid resolve. His voice shaking with emotion, he said, "Nine years ago you sent me off to the Army, and you're sending me off again."

"The Army showed you what you *didn't* want to do. Now find what you *do* want." Atan rose from his chair. "Let's talk inside where it's cooler."

The two walked along the veranda, their shadows glistening on the veneer of morning dew clinging to the siding of the house.

# THREE

$Z$AINE AND HIS FATHER ENTERED THE HOUSE. They passed the splashing waters of a fountain in the center of the foyer, making the cool dampness ideal for the hanging ferns and orchids, then down the hall to the kitchen.

Zaine was 27 years old now, tall and lean with a shock of black hair that fell over his forehead. His coloring was that of a perfect tan; the result of an American mother and a Malaysian father. His mother had been a professional singer on a world tour in an operetta. Her costume had torn on a scenery nail during a performance in Kuala Lumpur, and a tailor, Atan Nasir, was called. As soon as they met an unlikely romance began: the singer and the tailor, the American and the Malaysian. After a year of correspondence, Atan came to America, married Naomi, and settled in her hometown of Fall River, Massachusetts, a formidable textile city. The following year Zaine was born.

Choosing a name for their son proved difficult. Atan wanted it to be Malay, Naomi argued for an American name. Atan offered Omar, Zaine, and Ramli. Naomi suggested Bob, Charles, and Harold. After a long discussion, Naomi accepted the name Zaine. The more she said it aloud the more it appealed to her—like a cowboy's name suggesting a free spirit and strong will.

Zaine pulled a chair from the kitchen table and sat down. He ran his thumbnail along one of the many relief marks in the dark wood while Atan brought fresh fruit and two plates to the table then went back to the kitchen drawer for two paring knives. Zaine watched his father. He recalled coming back from the Army after boot camp and noticed that his father's demeanor had changed. The always-smiling face he remembered as a child now reflected the sadness of losing Naomi.

When Zaine was in high school, his mother was diagnosed with Cancer. Shockingly, in five months she was gone. He passed through his high school years in a lack luster daze. His father was well aware of the state he was in and after Zaine graduated had said, "You've got to get away. You need to find some stimulation."

"What do you want me to do?"

"Join the Army."

"The Army?" he said somewhat flabbergasted.

"Yes, go and see the recruiter."

He recalled the thrill and excitement he felt racing home to tell his father he had signed up. Thirteen weeks later, after completing boot camp, he came home on leave. He was eager to show off his uniform to his father but was stunned by what he saw when he entered the house. The window curtains had been taken down and boxes filled the living room.

"Dad, what's going on?" his voice echoing in the near-empty room.

"I'm moving back to Malaysia."

He never dreamt his father would want to return to his birthplace. It had never been discussed. "Why would you want to do that?" he asked.

Atan told him that with Naomi gone and Zaine away, he would do something he always wanted to do: manufacture his own shirts. Fall River's textile mills had awakened this passion in him.

Zaine felt disoriented. His home would now be somewhere far away from Fall River, far away from *America*. He had nothing to hold onto—he was uprooted physically and emotionally.

Zaine was assigned to Fort Ord, California. He liked the Army until a Sergeant ordered him to dig blades of grass out of the cracks in the sidewalk. Then and there any thoughts of a military career vanished.

He left the Army as a Corporal and traveled across the Pacific for the first look at his new home in a new country. His father met him at the airport in Kuala Lumpur, and they made the two-hour drive north to Batupura. Atan had bought property that included a little cottage with a connecting path to the main house. The cottage was for Zaine.

Several years later two things happened: he learned to manage a shirt factory, and he fell in love with Rayna. She dazzled him. But now she had cut into his comfort zone and handed him a slice of reality. *"You cannot truly live without a passion for the work you do in life."*

Atan sat down, selected a mango from the bowl of fruit and began to slice it.

"So what's next, father?" said Zaine petulantly.

Atan ignored his son's tone. "I'm giving you the freedom to find your passion in life. Freedom to go *any*where to find it, and with good fortune you *will* find it. Start tomorrow morning."

Zaine was ambivalent about leaving. He knew his father's business had stalled. Sales were dropping despite the uniqueness and high quality of the Malaysian designs his father created. "If I leave now, you'll be out of business before I get back."

"I'll worry about keeping the business alive," he said.

"You're dreaming," said Zaine insolently.

"If it weren't for a dream the factory wouldn't be here in the first place," said Atan with finality.

"But Dad, be realistic. Where's the money to pay for this?"

Atan smiled broadly. "That's the good news. During your mother's illness we decided to take some of our savings and set it aside for you for a special occasion. It's ten thousand dollars." Atan rose from the table and went to his room returning moments later with an envelope. "Here, Zaine."

27

Zaine looked at the envelope. *To my dear son, Zaine,* it said. The mucilage had dried, and the flap popped open with little effort. He slowly pulled out the letter.

*Dearest Zaine,*

*I know your father must believe this is a very special time in your life for you to read my letter.*

*Perhaps you are getting married; perhaps a child is on the way. I couldn't begin to imagine how you will use the money we saved. Your father and I agreed it would be used for something big, something grand.*

*Zaine, my son, I will be celebrating your joy with you in whatever you apply this gift to.*

*With everlasting love,*

*Mother*

Tears welled up in his eyes. He could not speak. Finally, "Thank you, father," he managed.

Zaine folded the letter carefully and inserted it back into the envelope. It was so quiet he could hear the water splashing in the foyer fountain and the buzz of cicadas outside. With his voice barely audible, Zaine said, "Where shall I begin?"

"There's an old woman who lives south of here," said Atan leaning back in his chair, "that I believe could help you get started. "Her name is Mara Hashimi. She's traveled all over the world as a governess for some very successful families."

"When did you meet her?"

"I was invited to her retirement party several years ago—when you were in the Army. Very engaging lady. Perhaps her experiences and insight will give you some direction."

"And where exactly do I find her?"

"About fifteen miles south, you'll see a series of swing bridges on your right spanning a muddy stream. She lives by the third bridge. Cross over the bridge and ask for Mara Hashimi."

They both stood. Atan faced his son, took him by the shoulders and said, "Zaine, back in Fall River I saw too many people who hated their jobs, were disillusioned with their lives and didn't know what to do about it. Rayna and I don't want that to happen to you. Go now, and find the career meant for you." He drew him close and whispered, "I love you, son."

They hugged each other, and, feeling the release of his father's arms, Zaine turned and walked down the hall to the foyer. At the fountain he leaned over, scooped his hand into the water and splashed his face several times until he felt cool. Then he went outside into the steamy heat of Batupura.

As he followed the path to his cottage he asked himself, "What do I want to be when I grow up?" He was amused at the child-like nature of the question.

He remembered his mother asking him that same question. When he could not respond, she read him the Bible story of Bartemaeus, the blind man, who sat on the side of the road, lost in the multitude of people as the King of Kings passed. He called out, people tried to shush him; yet he called and called until he was heard. And because he called, his sight was restored. His mother concluded dramatically, "He's passing your way, Zaine, right now. Call out to Him. Tell Him what you want!" Zaine could not—not then.

But now, he looked skyward and desperately implored, "Please. Help me find the right career. A career I'll be passionate about!"

# FOUR

IN THE MORNING ZAINE put his suitcase into the trunk of his aging, silver Toyota then slid behind the wheel. He looked at his cottage through the windshield and wondered when he would return.

Looking off to the mountains, he thought of why people climb mountains and the universal answer: because they are there. He was climbing his own mountain to discover *what* was there.

A breeze ruffled the palm fronds making a raspy sound as they rubbed their silver tips, and he turned the key in the ignition. The engine clattered to life sending a plume of smoke through the exhaust. He backed out of his grass driveway to the paved road that would take him south to Mara Hashimi. The drive was familiar; a winding road with thick vegetation on either side. As each mile passed, an unexpected feeling of excitement surprised him.

Soon, he caught a glimpse of the muddy stream running parallel to the road. He spotted the first of the swing bridges his father spoke of, further on another, and finally, the third. He slowed and stopped.

He got out of his car, stretched, and headed for the little bridge. The bridge was nothing more than loose boards, warped by the sun, and placed on top of two by fours laid across two cables that stretched from bank to bank. It was inexpensive, crude, efficient. There was no railing, just a steel cable on either side to grab to keep from falling into the water. He found the going awkward. The boards popped up when he stepped on them causing him to lurch and lose his balance as the bridge swung sideways. He finally made his way across in a jerky half run, half walk. And there before him was a surprise: three exquisite houses, each with their own unique charm. He noticed a young woman in a bright floral dress standing on the porch of one of the houses. She smiled as he approached.

"Hello," said Zaine.

She responded with a nod.

"Could you tell me where Mara Hashimi lives?"

"Why certainly," she said. "It is here. I'm her niece."

"My name is Zaine Nasir. I'm from Batupura."

"I'm Azizah. Won't you come in, Zaine? Mara is inside." Azizah was a plain, ample woman with a round face and expressive brown eyes.

Zaine stepped onto the colorful floor of the living room, pink and magenta tiles with a yellow flower in each center. Bookshelves dominated an entire wall. Against another wall was a cushioned rattan sofa, and facing the sofa an old woman sat in a rocking chair smiling at him.

"This is my Aunt Mara," Azizah said.

"Hello," he said. "My name is Zaine."

"I'll get some cold juice for you, Zaine. Would you like some, too, Aunt Mara?"

"Please," she replied.

Azizah pushed through the curtain separating the living room from the dining room and hastened to the kitchen in the back of the house.

"My father told me to talk with you," said Zaine taking a seat on the sofa.

33

The old woman nodded as she rocked. She made several sounds as though clearing a passage somewhere between the back of her nose and throat. With her lips pressed together, she sent a rush of air from her nostrils culminating in a *k'hm* sound. Zaine dismissed it as a kind of audible tic. Its frequency was not unpleasant.

"Your father sent you?" she asked cordially.

Zaine nodded.

"Is he in government?"

"Oh, no," Zaine laughed. "He owns a shirt factory in Batupura. He was at your retirement party."

Mara said nothing as she rocked. Her salt and pepper hair was pulled back in a careless bun held by an ivory chopstick, her sole adornment. She wore a nondescript black dress incongruously complemented by the black swoosh on her white sneakers. The sparkle in her eyes indicated an active mind and perhaps a sense of humor. He guessed she was in her eighties.

Azizah returned with the cold drinks and took her seat on the sofa with Zaine.

"Thank you, Azizah," he said taking a sip.

Mara pressed the cold glass to her cheek. "Why did your father send you to me, Zaine?"

"He said because you've traveled so much you might be able to help me. You were a governess?"

"That's true. I've lived all over the world. *k'hm*. I loved being a governess," she said taking a rather large gulp of juice. "I was with one family for five years. He was a writer. Liked to write people stories."

Zaine brightened, captivated by the reedy timbre in her voice as she rocked back and forth, her sneakers providing excellent traction.

"We went to Spain where he wrote about a midget toreador. Bravest thing I ever saw. *El Enano Torero*. In his costume of red and gold, he stood eye level with the bull. Every time the bull charged him the crowd would gasp, but always he darted out of the way just in time."

Zaine could imagine the bull's hot breath on the little man's face and the flying spittle.

"And when it was over, the crowd threw flowers at *El Enano*. Amidst cheers and applause, men dashed from the stands and carried him on their shoulders out of the ring. Now *there* was a man who wanted to be big, and a toreador in Pamplona is about as big as you can get."

"That's a great story," Zaine said. "He found what he wanted to do in life. That's exactly what my father wants me to find—what I want to find." His excitement grew as he added, "That's why I'm here."

"You want *me* to find what you are supposed to do in life? You came here for *that*?" Mara ceased rocking and said directly, "*You're* the one who is supposed to figure that out!"

Her sharpness startled Zaine, but recovering quickly he asked, "How did you discover that your passion was to be a governess?"

"Oh, that goes a way back," she said, a smile playing around her lips.

*K'hm.* "When I was very young, living here in Malaysia, I came across a National Geographic Magazine. It showed places far away from here, and I instantly wanted to visit them. I wanted to travel, Zaine. Always did. One day, when I was working as an information clerk at a hotel in Kuala Lumpur, an American sailor came up to my booth. As soon as I laid eyes on him, I fell in love. He walked right up and asked me . . .," she paused and laughed. "I don't remember what he asked me to tell you the truth, he was so darned good looking." She and Azizah giggled. "I hardly heard a word he said. We had a marvelous time during his stay. I hated to see him leave. Several months later he wrote to me from America and asked me to come to Newport, Rhode Island, where he lived. He paid for my fare—on a sailor's pay no less!"

"And you went?"

"Yes, against my parent's wishes. Very tearful scene, my leaving was, but it was my first opportunity to travel. Took forever to get to Providence, Rhode Island where he was supposed to meet me. He wasn't there when I arrived. I called his home. His parents said he was out to sea, and they didn't know anything about my coming to visit. How's that!" She rocked in silence for a moment.

"But why?"

"Who knows *why?* Cold feet I guess. Who knows," she added wistfully as she continued rocking.

Zaine watched her eyes. Her focus drifted recalling that time long ago.

"Anyway," she continued, "I found a place to stay and took as many jobs as I could. I hired out as a baby sitter, clerked at a department store and waitressed at a restaurant until I had enough money to take some college courses. And you know what I discovered when I got to college? I liked languages. And of all the jobs I had, I found being with children the most fulfilling. When you put it together—travel, languages, children—I was perfectly suited to be a governess."

The ease with which Mara spoke and her lack of pretense was such that Zaine felt comfortable enough to share a private matter of the heart.

"I have a confession," he said impulsively. "The urgency to find my passion came because of this letter from the woman I love. I received it the day after I proposed to her." He removed the letter from his pocket.

Both women came to attention. Azizah's brown eyes widened, Mara emitted a *k'hm*. "Zizi, more juice please. Make a pitcher."

"Surely," said Azizah quickly rising from the sofa. "Zaine, don't say a word until I get back," she ordered as she left the room.

To counter the silence Zaine asked Mara, "Did you ever marry?"

"Came close, Zaine. Close a couple of times," she laughed. "My mother told me to marry a man

38

whose faults I could live with. Well, I concentrated on the faults of every man I met and threw them all out!" Her laugh was hearty. His visit had given her day a lift. *k'hm.*

Azizah hurriedly returned with the pitcher and set it on the table. Zaine walked the letter over to Mara. Zizi went behind the rocking chair to peer over Mara's shoulder, and they both began to read. Zaine poured a glassful of juice and sat down.

When they finished Mara said, "Well, now. Here's a woman mature beyond her years. You're a lucky man, Zaine. Rayna knows what passion is, but I don't think you do," she said, her voice rising. "Passion is the strongest emotion you can feel. I can't tell you what you're suppose to do in life, but I will tell you what others have said when they found a career they were passionate about.

"I knew a woman who was in construction. I asked her how she chose that field. It was something you didn't figure a woman would be drawn to. You know what she said? She said, 'I love it so much, I even love the *smell* of it'. Now, that's passion!

"Azizah always knew she wanted to be a school teacher. Tell him why, Zizi."

"I wouldn't feel complete doing anything else."

"See there?" said Mara. "She wouldn't be *complete* unless she was teaching. That's passion! Now, on the other hand, listen to what happens when someone *doesn't* find their passion. I once was the governess for the son of a wealthy stockbroker in New Jersey. From the time he was born, his life was already planned by his parents. He would attend a prep school, go to college and from there to a fine position in a large corporation. And that he did. I get a card from him every so often. He sent one about four years ago. Azizah, in the drawer of my nightstand is the card from Curtis. Bring it out for me would you please?"

Azizah hustled back through the dividing curtain and returned handing the card to Mara.

"Yes, this is the one. Listen to what he wrote. *'I think of you often with joy and respect.'* Zaine, this is some 40 years later!"

"You must have made a great impression."

"He was a lovely boy. But there's a sadness here. Listen to what else he says. *'I still don't know what I want to do when I grow up'.* Zaine, the man is a vice-president of a power company. He was 51 years old when he sent this! His

40

parents robbed him of the opportunity to think about what *he* wanted to do in life. They stole his future! His *life!*" Her voice rose, and a sneaker burp started the rocker in motion. "He was never allowed, or had the mind-set, to try new things. Don't be afraid to do that. It shows you're alive."

"Well, I'm certainly alive," he mumbled.

"No, Zaine, you've been existing up there in Batupura, not living. You thought you were living, but you were not. I had some gallstones removed once. I was in, oh, what do you call it?"

"Hospital?" said Azizah.

"No, not hospital. Of course I was in the hospital. It's where they put you after surgery. The, ah . . ."

"Intensive care un—"

"Intensive care unit, right," she continued. "They have you hooked up to a machine that shows the patterns of your heartbeat on a monitor. If your heart stops, all you see is a straight line. Some people's lives are a straight line. They never experience *passion*."

Zaine realized his life in Batupura had been a straight line, and Rayna's letter was the shock he needed.

"But now, dear boy, you *are* starting to live. Where are you going after you leave here?"

Before he could answer Mara said, "Go to America. The Americans are the risk takers. You're an American. You ought to know that. Find out why in a free society everyone isn't doing what he or she loves to do—was *born* to do." *k'hm.*

As they made their goodbyes Mara whispered, "Don't forget *El Enano Torero*—the brave little man who would risk death to live his passion." Azizah held the door open, while Zaine thanked Mara, and joined him as he walked to the bridge.

"Azizah, is there something wrong with me that I don't know what my career should be?"

"Not at all, Zaine." She put her arm in his and said, "Some of us just need a little more time to get where we're going."

"I guess I'll take Mara's advice and go to America," he said.

"Where in America?" she asked.

"San Francisco."

"Why there?"

"It's closest to home," he laughed. "Seriously, I was stationed there in the Army. I know the city."

At the bridge, Zaine thanked her and crossed over the muddy stream—this time taking longer strides to prevent the bridge from yawing. He got into his car and continued to Kuala Lumpur, where he would take the flight to San Francisco.

As he drove, he thought of the people that Mara spoke of who had found their niche in life. But he was frustrated because she didn't tell him *how* they found it, and *how* did they recognize it when they found it?

But what Mara did make absolutely clear to him was that life was only complete when you found what you were born to do. Zaine knew that he must find a career he was passionate about or his life would be *in*complete—empty . . . as empty as a home without Rayna.

# FIVE

THE BOEING 744 ROARED DOWN THE RUNWAY, soared over the purple mountains of Malaysia and headed for San Francisco.

Before leaving he had written two postcards; one to his father . . .

*Dear Dad,*

*Meeting with Mara went well. She's quite a character. I'm flying to the States.*

*Dad, I know how much you love being in the factory and how you hate to solicit business, but please don't let sales slip. It worries me.*

*I'll call you from San Francisco.*

*Love,*

*Your son*

And to Rayna . . .

*Hey Rayn,*

*I'm on my way to America to discover my elusive "passion." I don't know what I'll find or when I'll return, but I'm very excited. Hope your meeting in Hong Kong went well. Miss you—*

*Love ya,*

*Z.*

He wished Rayna was with him, that they could take this trip together, but he realized that some things you have to do alone. He thought of the irony of his mission—going farther away from Rayna to be closer to her.

The cabin lights dimmed so passengers might get some sleep. He sighed and turned his thoughts to his future. Would he work in an office? Would he be a mechanic, a pilot, a salesman? Would he go to school as Mara had and take subjects his heart led him to? He ticked off job titles with the hope that somehow just mentioning the occupation would magically kindle a fire of passion within. No passion stirred.

He recalled Mara's last words to him. *'Find out why in a free society everyone isn't doing what they love to do—were born to do.'*

He smiled at the logic. Yet, as he settled his head into the pillow, a wave of insecurity came over him. It was daunting to look for something he had never been able to find before. He thought, if I was looking for a needle in a hay stack, I'd at least know what I was looking for.

## SIX

He arrived in San Francisco at dawn and taxied to the Marriott. A room was available, and he immediately went up to it and slept.

At two in the afternoon he was in the coffee shop mulling over what his first action should be. The very *first* thing he needed was some clothes.

The concierge helped him rent a car and, since he was familiar with San Francisco, he knew exactly where to find Nordstrom's.

Driving downtown, he once again marveled at the steep hills and smiled at the artful way the motormen rang the bell on their cable cars.

When he walked into the men's department of Nordstrom's, Zaine was astonished at the size of the manufacturer's displays: Ralph Lauren, Izod, Nautica, Tommy Hilfiger, and others. They were all much larger than he'd recalled five years ago. The most compelling display was that of Michael Leonardi. The focal point of Leonardi's collection was a lion's head—an actual close-up photograph of the king of the jungle—the Leonardi logo. The lion logo was everywhere.

Zaine picked up a shirt and examined the workmanship and feel of the cloth as his father had taught him. But when he read the label, he stopped cold. The shirt he held was finished in Taiwan. He picked up several others and noted they were made in other countries as well.

Suddenly, a thought occurred to him. Why not make them in Malaysia? *We* could make shirts for Michael Leonardi, he thought. He bought a shirt and asked the clerk where Leonardi's offices were. She told him New York City. He ran to his car and drove to the hotel.

In his room, he immediately picked up the phone, called information and then connected with the offices of Michael Leonardi only to have a recorded message tell him the offices were closed. He'd forgotten about the three hour time difference between the East and West coasts.

In Batupura it was morning. His father would be up. He called him.

"Good morning, father. I'm in San Francisco."

"Good morning, son. How was your trip? Have you found something that—"

"Dad, listen. I've an idea. I just came from a department store. You should see all the shirts from all the manufacturers. And they're not all made in the United States. I never noticed that before. I mean I saw the labels a hundred times, but it never clicked until now. These shirts are made in Taiwan, Jamaica, and Mexico, and I'm thinking maybe we could make these at our place in Malaysia. What do you think?"

Atan remained silent.

"Father?"

"Yes, I'm here. I'm thinking. You want to make shirts for someone else at our facilities?"

"Sure. Why not?"

"Why would I want to do that?" said Atan. "Why would we want to work for someone else?"

Zaine had not thought of it as giving up independence but as maintaining independence.

"What's wrong with a little diversifying?" he responded. "Look, *some*body's making money making shirts for these big guys, why not us, too?"

"Who do you have in mind?"

51

"Leonardi. Father, he has the best display you've ever seen. A huge photograph of a lion dominates the entire men's department. Every shirt has a lion logo on it. It's everywhere."

"So what you're suggesting is two businesses?"

"Exactly. Our own brand that we make and the other business making  shirts for someone else. It would give us a steady base of income." He paused then added, "We need that, Dad."

"He might reject us because of our size, but the quality of our shirts might attract him. What did the shirts look like that you saw?"

"The sewing wasn't spectacular, but there was a nice feel to the fabric."

Atan smiled. "Wait 'til he sees ours. You'll need some samples to show him."

"I'll make hotel reservations in New York and call you back with the address. Bye, father."

"Zaine, wait a minute. How are you coming on your career search?"

"Dad, let me see this through first. If I can swing this, you won't ever have to go on a sales call again! You'd like that, right?"

"True," he smiled. "Now, son, remember a lot of Americans still think Malaysians carry baskets on their heads, so pick a good hotel in New York. Stay at a *fine* one, son. Goodbye."

Zaine could not see the broad smile on his father's face as he hung up the phone.

## SEVEN

IN THE MORNING HE DRESSED and went downstairs for breakfast. The coffee shop was filled with conventioneers occupying most of the tables. He found a single and observed the group.

"Pardon me," he said to the man at the next table. "What convention is this?"

"It's a sales conference."

"I see," said Zaine. "And what do you do?"

The man looked at Zaine for a moment. "We sell," he said dryly before breaking into a laugh.

"Really."

The man explained. "There's about two thousand of us here in the hotel from all over the country. We meet and compare notes—how to get clients, how to keep 'em, stuff like that. What brings you to San Francisco?"

Zaine didn't want to go into his real purpose with a stranger, so he said, "Just coming back to see the city again. I was stationed here in the Army. By the way, my name is Zaine Nasir."

"Mine's Bill Gifford. Pleased to meet you. Zaine, have you ever heard of a guy named Roy Hawkins? Ever hear him speak?"

Zaine gave him a blank look.

Gifford continued, "He's kicking off our opening session." He looked at his watch. "The session starts in about 10 minutes."

"What does he talk about?" asked Zaine.

"Sales, son, sales and how to make more of them. Look, why don't you be my guest and hear this guy?"

"Well, I really shouldn't, I've got a phone call to make, but . . . what the heck. Sure."

"Good decision, kid. It isn't often you get to hear a guy like Roy Hawkins. Follow me," he said getting up from the table. "Everyone on the planet should hear this guy."

Zaine followed Bill out of the coffee shop to the convention wing of the hotel, curious as to why Gifford was so cranked up about seeing this Hawkins guy.

The buzz of conversation intensified as they neared the large hall where the salespeople were assembling. He could feel their energy as he walked among them. Is this how you feel when you've found your right career? He wondered.

They entered the auditorium and Bill Gifford found two seats about a third of the way from the stage on the left side. The lights dimmed, and a woman came to the microphone at the center of the stage. She introduced Mr. Hawkins as one who had a humble beginning, failed many times in life, but finally found success selling products door to door. From that experience he developed a "monster" business. She told of how one day someone asked Mr. Hawkins his secret to success. It was then he created the Hawkins Success System: a system that would help anyone achieve "unbelievable" riches. "May I present—Mr. Roy Haww-kinnns."

To enthusiastic applause, Roy Hawkins dashed from the wings to center stage. He bussed his introducer on the cheek and raised his arms wide to the audience, which increased the applause Zaine noted. He wore gray slacks, a blue blazer with a crest, and his white shirt was French cuffed. His bright yellow tie was held by a diamond pin that flashed in the spotlight. Zaine was wide-eyed. He's like a movie star, he thought.

Roy Hawkins paced, deep in thought it appeared. He looked up at the ceiling as though searching for and *receiving* a message. He whipped the microphone out of its stand effortlessly, snapped the cord, and with barely a whisper said, "Do you know why so many people fail in life?"

The crowd was still. He looked over the audience letting the suspense build. "Because they don't have a system," he said in a breathy stage whisper. Then he startled the audience by shouting in a slow cadence, "THEY—DON'T—HAVE—A—SYSTEM!"

Returning to his normal voice he said, "I'm going to give you a system that I guarantee—if you apply it—will make you a winner." A buzz ran through the audience as they anticipated the secrets that Roy Hawkins would reveal. Zaine was captivated.

In the hour-long presentation, Roy Hawkins told his story. What it was like growing up poor. His first sales call. His first failure. His ultimate success all because he developed a system. He used slides to show photographs of his life. The first showed him as a little boy sitting on an old tractor. The last picture showed him relaxing on his yacht, *Euphoria*. He spun story after story, some funny, some heartbreaking. Zaine thought he was magic.

He told of how in the first grade that Miss Wilde had given him a 'D' in art. "How could anyone give a first grader a 'D' in art?" he asked. "I was only six years old! How dare she judge me, scar me, put me down like that. For years and years, even into my adult years, I truly believed I was worthless in art.

"How many of you were told you were a 'D' in something—no good, hopeless, don't even think about doing it, huh? Don't let anyone tell you that you can't do something. They have no right to do that. So clear the slate. This is a new day. You are terrific. You can do ANYTHING!!!" The crowd burst into applause. Zaine was applauding, too, eager to receive the important lessons of Mr. Hawkins' system.

Actually, the "important lessons" of his system were in his tape series that was on sale just outside the convention hall doors. But he did lay out the big picture, and Zaine didn't miss a word.

Hawkins talked first of having a vision.

"Once you have the *vision,* where you want to go, then you create the *plan.* Actuate the plan," he said, "and you'll begin to reap the *rewards.* After you've gone through all of the planning and good times and bad times to reap the profits, don't forget to have a *celebration.* You deserve it because you are worth it." He had the crowd chant with him. He would ask, "Why do you deserve it?" And they would respond, "Because I'm worth it."

When he finished, music from the sound system blared out a march. Roy Hawkins took his bows as the highly charged audience clapped in rhythm.

Outside the hall Zaine fought for his place in line amidst the frenzy of people eager to purchase his tapes. He lost Bill Gifford in the crush. With his Roy Hawkins' Success System album under his arm, he went up to his room, his adrenaline soaring.

He propped the album on the table in his room and sat on the edge of his bed looking at it. He thought of the word vision, the first step in Hawkins' system. Then it hit him. He couldn't begin until he *had* a vision. My god, am I blind to my own vision?

A vision, he reasoned, has to begin with a dream. But a high school teacher had once scolded, "Stop dreaming and get down to business." So he learned that to dream was a bad thing. He had even used that word when he told his father he was dreaming about getting new business. Yet his father's dream to open his own factory had become a reality. He himself dreamed of Rayna and envisioned a family with her; that didn't seem unrealistic. He dreamed of meeting Leonardi in New York City. Was it unrealistic to envision that something good might come of this meeting? Yes, he decided, dreaming *was* a good thing; how else could a vision be born?

But he drew a blank as to what his dream was. He was back to square one. If only Hawkins had covered this situation in his speech. Was Hawkins still in the hotel? Could he talk with him personally—one on one? Would he? Zaine picked up the phone and called the front desk. He asked to be connected to Roy Hawkins.

"It's a great day to be alive! This is Roy."

Zaine was startled. Roy Hawkins on the phone was as exciting as seeing him on the stage.

"Hello, sir, my name is Zaine Nasir. I'm staying here at the same hotel. I just saw you this morning and bought your tapes, too."

"Well, thank you, Zaine. What can I do for you?"

"Well, uh," he paused gathering the courage to ask his next question. "Could I see you? I, uh, I have a problem with your tapes."

"Defective are they?"

"Oh, I, well I don't know. I haven't heard them yet."

Hawkins said nothing so Zaine stammered on. "I don't believe I can start using your information because . . . this sounds stupid, but I don't have a vision." Zaine laughed nervously. "You said you have to start with a vision, and I don't have one." His voice trailed off. Then, meekly, "so you see I can't put your system into practice."

There was a lengthy pause at the other end of the line. Finally, Hawkins said, "Can you be in my room in five minutes?"

Zaine brightened. "Yes, sir."

"I'm up in the penthouse. Twenty-three-ten."

"I'm on my way."

# EIGHT

ZAINE GRABBED THE HAWKINS' ALBUM and headed down the hall. A short wait for the elevator, and he ascended to the 23rd floor. Hawkins greeted him at the door.

"Zaine, come in," he said with a hearty handshake. "Have a seat," nodding to the sofa. He had removed his blue blazer revealing a crisp white shirt and wide yellow suspenders. He sat in the wing chair across from Zaine. "We haven't much time, Zaine. I have to catch a plane. We've only about 20 minutes."

Zaine tried to calm his emotions that danced from the excitement of being in Hawkins' presence to his desperation for a system to get him unstuck.

Hawkins opened. "You said on the phone you have no vision of what you want to do in life."

63

"Correct," said Zaine. "Let me tell you why this search is so important to me. I'm an American, but I live in Malaysia with my father and work at his factory. He's a shirt maker. Last week I proposed to the woman I want to marry. She said if I continued to work at the factory, I'd eventually be bored and unhappy because I have no passion for the work. She told me to look around and find a career I'd be passionate about.

"Hearing you this morning got me excited. But when I got back to my room, I realized that I can't start to apply anything you said because I have no vision. Mr. Hawkins, I've *never* had a vision of a career that I'd be passionate about. Has anyone else come to you with this sort of problem?"

Zaine caught a smile on Hawkins' face. Their eyes met. Zaine didn't know what to ask next. He didn't have to.

"Zaine, do you know how many people I meet with the same problem? Hundreds," he said as he rose from his chair and walked to the window to gaze at the San Francisco skyline. Without looking at Zaine he casually asked, "What brought you to San Francisco?"

"A woman in Malaysia suggested it, thought my career chances were better in the States. She

64

asked me to find out why in a free society like America everyone isn't doing what they want to do."

Hawkins turned to him. "What a great question. That's good. I'll have to use that in my speeches. I'll bet half the people in the United States aren't doing what they'd like to do. Just like you, they're visionless." He returned his gaze to the skyline, his thumb hooked casually under a suspender.

Zaine offered a smile. "Do you have a kind of, ah, guide to help people like us?"

Hawkins turned taking a deep breath. "Yes, I do," he said. "Getting ready to introduce it. That's why I invited you to come up. Want to test it."

Zaine brightened. Hawkins looked at his watch. "We can talk while I pack."

"Great," said Zaine. "I really appreciate this."

"Glad to do it," he said with a nonchalant wave of his hand as they walked down the short hallway to the bedroom. Zaine took a seat at the table by the window while Hawkins brought his garment bag from the closet, laid it on the bed, and proceeded to pack.

"Do you always travel alone?" asked Zaine surprised that he didn't have an entourage.

"Only when I have a one-shot like this. I bring my wife when I'm asked to conduct a three-day conference—especially when they're held at a nice resort, which most of them are."

"I see," said Zaine.

Hawkins unzipped a compartment in his garment bag. "Now let's focus on you. First of all, Zaine, you've got it backwards. You're not blind to your vision, you're blind to your gift. You can't focus on a career until you know what your gift is. That's the link to your passion.

"Gift?"

"Yes. What are you good at? Everybody's good at something."

Zaine sighed and slumped down in the chair.

Hawkins read his body language and responded, "Now, don't get discouraged. Think of someone you know who has discovered their gift, then linked it to their passion and turned it into a career."

Immediately, Zaine thought of his father. It was obvious. His gift was the ability to design and sew beautiful shirts. His passion was to manufacture these shirts, and it became his career the day he built his factory.

Hawkins folded several neckties and placed them into the designated compartment of his garment bag. "You know what's odd about our gift? Others can see it plain as day. It's so obvious to them they assume we know it, too. But we don't. We say, 'How could this be anything special when it's so easy—second nature—to us?' We take it for granted and stupidly make the assumption that anyone can do what we do. We downplay the word 'gift' as it applies to us. We think it's a lofty word that only applies to artists—painters, musicians, sculptors. Let me tell you something, Zaine. Every one of us has been endowed with something that we're good at doing, and that *some*thing is our special gift. We're born with it and cannot change it."

In his life Zaine had never thought about what he was good at. Furthermore, no one *ever* pointed out any special talent in him. "How do I determine what I'm good at?" he asked eagerly.

"Let me give you a little personal background so you'll understand how my method works. The first thing I did was analyze my career by *accessing my past*. I wondered what led me to do what I was doing. Accessing your past is a process of taking the time to really go back in your life to dig up and find all the moments in which you were doing something you absolutely loved to do. I realized my love, my passion, was to communicate and persuade people. I loved presenting to people, and I wanted a bigger audience. I asked the company if I could speak at their year-end sales conference. Lots of people were there at that conference, lots. The first time I stepped on the stage and talked to them? Bam! I knew I was in the right place. Right church, right pew. I loved everything about it. It was far more thrilling than presenting to Mom and Pop in their home. This was big stuff—the lights, the stage, the anticipation of speaking to a large group of people, the excitement of it. Whew!

"I realized I could affect the emotions of the people I was speaking to. Zaine, I could make them laugh or cry, but it was only when they profited by something I said that I was validated, fulfilled. My gift is my ability to communicate, persuade and emotionally impact people. That's what I learned about myself when I *accessed* my past.

The second part of my method is to *act* on my gift. I did that by speaking to large groups of people. See Zaine? I'd linked my gift with my passion and carved out a career for myself. *Access your past* to find your gift, *act on your gift* to find your career.

"When you act on your gift you gain tremendous confidence in yourself, and your self-esteem soars sky high. And it's all validated when you use your gift to serve others—in my case with a Success System. It's what you heard this morning and what I recorded in my album. Vision, Plan, Reward, Celebration."

Zaine could only sit and stare at Roy Hawkins. He was just as mesmerizing in person as he was on stage.

Hawkins spoke softly now, "Zaine, I thought I'd found the Holy Grail. But you know what happened? The media tagged me the 'feel-good' man. Said I pumped up audiences with a lot of motivational talk that wore off after a couple of days. Here I am bustin' my chops, giving audiences a system for success—giving them my heart and soul—and I'm accused of being a 'feel-good' man. That's like saying I'm a charlatan. That hurt. I asked myself, 'What am I leaving out'? You know what I found out?"

Zaine blurted, "No, what?"

"The same thing that you found out. My message was falling on a lot of deaf ears. What good is a Success System for people who don't know where they're going? It was then I realized I wouldn't be *totally* fulfilled until I could offer something that would help every person in the audience."

He slapped his fist into the palm of his hand. "Whoooaa, Zaine," he shouted. "If I can help people *access their gift* and *act on that gift,* they'd be led to a career they'd be passionate about for the rest of their lives! Wouldn't *that* be something? Add my Success System to that, and there's no telling how far they can go."

Zaine stared, transfixed by Roy Hawkins. "Help me begin," he asked urgently.

Hawkins looked at his watch. "We haven't much time, Zaine, so let's access your past and see what pops up. Are you ready?"

Zaine nodded, "Yes, sir."

"Tell me about three episodes in your life when you were involved in something that made you happy. Three occasions. That's all. Three things that you've enjoyed doing in your life."

Zaine, without much thought, said, "Well, I was in the Army."

"Did you enjoy it?"

"I did at the start, but then—"

"Stop! Why did you like it at the start?"

"I liked the regimentation, the challenges. That sort of thing."

"Did you like working with others?"

"Oh, yes, that was fun."

"Fun or easy for you?"

"Both. I liked getting people together to accomplish whatever we were assigned. I liked building a team."

Hawkins nodded approvingly. "Go on," he said.

Zaine thought for a moment. "At my father's factory I was able to make the manufacturing process more streamlined, more productive. I liked doing that. I also came up with an incentive plan for the shirt makers and cutters."

"Why?" asked Roy Hawkins.

"So they would work as a team."

"What motivated you to do that?"

"Just seemed like common sense."

Hawkins nodded his head several times. He retrieved the few items he had in the bureau drawer and stuffed them in his garment bag. Then he sat opposite Zaine at the table.

"It seemed like common sense you say?"

"Yes. Doesn't it to you?"

71

Hawkins smiled, "Yes, but I wouldn't call it that in your case. I'd call it instinctive. Am I right? I mean you didn't spend a second analyzing the situation. You were following your instincts—your natural ability to organize and develop."

"Well, yes. So—"

"So just think what that says about you." He paused letting that resonate with Zaine. "Give me a third episode in your life where you did something that made you happy. Go back to when you were a kid. What's your earliest recollection of something you did that was totally enjoyable to you?"

"Does it have to be a job I had?"

"No, just tell me about something you did that was fun for you, something that was so enjoyable you remember it to this day."

Zaine smiled. "You're going to laugh at this, but my best memory was when I got the neighborhood kids involved in putting on our own Olympics.

"We were around 9 or 10 years old and inspired by watching the real Olympics on TV. I organized all the kids—must have been 15 of us. Each had a responsibility—make flags, make uniforms, which were white T-shirts with the name of the country they represented. One event was the triathlon. You had to run around the block, then bicycle around the block, and finally swim a couple of laps in a rich kid's pool. We even had an opening parade. One of the kids had a boombox that we set on the lawn, and the music blared away as we marched down the street. I led the parade, arms outstretched, holding up a sign that read Fall River Olympics. I loved doing that!"

Hawkins glanced at his watch, stood up, and went into the bathroom to gather his toiletries. He smiled as he returned and said, "Zaine, you've just completed the first step in my method. *Access.* You have dug up from your past what you've enjoyed doing most in your life. What you've told me about the Olympics, about helping your father's business, the specific things you told me about your Army experiences, has leads me to believe you have a gift for organization. You like to organize and build."

As they walked back to the living room, Zaine thought, organize and build? What the heck kind of unique gift is that? Everyone organizes stuff. And as for building? I just don't see it. The visit was proving to be a disappointment.

73

Hawkins glanced again at his watch. "We're out of time. Zaine, we've rushed through this process—the process of accessing your past. Think of more episodes in your life that you enjoyed. In fact, ask your father about things he noticed as you grew up. See if he could spot the gifts in you even then."

"We've never had a talk like that," said Zaine.

"I guess most parents don't." Hawkins paused looking down at the floor soberly. "Wouldn't it be helpful if parents *looked* for those special gifts in us and *told* us about them? How much easier it would be to know what we're *really* good at. That would help us clarify what we wanted to be when we grew up." Again he paused, nodding his head while looking directly at Zaine. "Now, let me ask you something. When you leave my room, what's the first thing you're going to do?"

"Well," he said slowly, "before I focus on me, I want to do something for my father. He's not the greatest businessman. Yesterday, I saw displays of shirts at Nordstrom's department store. They were manufactured in places like Mexico, Taiwan, and Jamaica. I thought maybe we could do the same thing for some company at our place in Malaysia. I was attracted to Leonardi's display, and I thought I'd follow through on that."

"Meaning?"

"If I could show Leonardi the quality of our shirts, maybe he'd hire us. That would give us a steady income base."

Hawkins smiled. "Doing this for your father?"

"Correct."

"It has nothing to do with you? You're sure of that?"

"Absolutely. I don't want to be a tailor like him."

"You're not crazy about the shirt business, I take it."

"Supervising a factory of people hunched over sewing machines? I don't think so. Dad's the one with the passion for making shirts, and I'm just trying to help him out."

"I think that's excellent, even noble of you, Zaine. Yes sir, you follow through on that." Changing the subject Hawkins said, "You brought my album with you. Would you like me to sign it?"

"Oh, certainly," said Zaine pleased at the thought. Roy signed it and handed it back to him.

"And here's my business card. Promise me you'll let me know how you make out. Tell me if my method has been helpful. What you discover could help me help others." Hawkins concluded, "Now that you know your gift, Zaine, you have the vision to find your career."

Zaine took his card and thanked him.

Down in the lobby, Zaine walked around reflecting on his meeting. *Access your gift. Act on your gift.* His lips moved as he repeated over and over: *access and act.* A mantra. He thought of what Hawkins said his gift was—to organize and develop. He shook his head, he didn't like his gift. He could see no real use for it—it seemed hardly anything special enough to even be called a gift.

He stopped at the hotel's souvenir shop and looked at the display in the window. A tiny replica of a San Francisco cable car caught his eye. He went in and bought it for Rayna. He wondered what she'd think if he told her what Hawkins said about him. They'd probably have a good laugh. Roy was a kind man, and Zaine appreciated the time he spent sharing his simplistic method. It just hadn't connected with him.

Back in his room, he placed the call to Leonardi's in New York. When the receptionist answered, he asked to speak to the person responsible for contracting foreign companies to make shirts for Leonardi's.

"Hello, Roger Burdick."

"Yes, Mr. Burdick. This is Zaine Nasir. I'm calling from San Francisco, but I live in Malaysia. We have a shirt factory there, and I was wondering if I could talk with you about manufacturing shirts for your company."

"Are you coming to New York?"

"Yes."

"Call me when you're in town."

"Could I set up an appointment now?"

"What's your name again?"

"Zaine Nasir."

"Call me when you get here, Mr. Nasir."

"I'll call you in a couple of days?"

"Fine."

Zaine hung up the phone. The conversation wasn't what he expected. It was too short. Yet, Burdick *did* tell him to call when in New York, so he quickly focused on what he would say to him once he arrived. His excitement at the prospect of selling their services to Leonardi grew while the conversation with Hawkins faded.

# NINE

**H**IS FLIGHT TO NEW YORK took five hours and twenty minutes. A taxi whisked him into Manhattan and deposited him at 118 West 57th Street, le Parker-Meridien Hotel. Exiting the taxi, he felt his pulse beat faster; he was captivated by the overwhelming energy and pace of the city.

Entering the breathtaking lobby with its white marble flooring and black accent squares, he looked up at the pillared balcony all the way to the top of the lobby's three story atrium.

At the registration desk, he asked if there was a package for him.

"Yes, Mr. Nasir, you have a package."

He registered, and the bellman took him to his room, a room with a perfect view of Central Park. It oozed of relaxed elegance: yellow and cream striped wallpaper, antique rose drapes, and a gold quilted bedspread with soft yellow throw pillows. His father would be pleased at his choice of such a *fine* hotel.

He carefully opened the package from Malaysia, and there, nestled in the tissue paper, was a note from Rayna. A surprise! He lifted the sealed flap with two fingers.

*Dearest Zaine,*

*I'm writing because it makes me feel close to you. I'm eager to hear what you're doing, what you're thinking about. I can't wait to see you.*

*I pray you'll find something you're so passionate about doing that I'll be jealous.*

*I think of you often . . . and then I think about you some more.*

*All my love,*

*Rayna*

Ah, to be close to Rayna right now. He pictured her tall, thin body. He loved to look at her face with its high cheek bones, her hazel eyes, and a smile that flat-out lit up his world. Her candor was the foundation of the trust they shared.

When Rayna was at the University of Hong Kong, he visited her. She had an apartment in Kowloon on the mainland of China, and each morning they took the ferry across Victoria Bay to her school. He loved those trips: the glow of the sun on her face, the salty smell of the morning breeze, the sound of the water splashing against the prow of the ferry as the steady pulse of the diesel engines powered them toward the imposing buildings sparkling in the sunshine against the backdrop of Mount Victoria.

Now, as he looked out his hotel-room window, the backdrop was New York City. He thought, after I finish this business for my father, maybe, just maybe, somewhere out there—in this city that offers more opportunities than perhaps any other—I will find the career I'll love as passionately as I love Rayna.

# TEN

**T**HE ELEVATOR DOORS CLOSED, and he was on his way up to the offices of Michael Leonardi. Under his arm he carried the box containing two sample shirts. When the doors opened, he stepped out into a stunning reception area. Plants and paintings all around, all exquisite and made more so by the soft sound of a waterfall in one corner. As he walked across the rich Oriental rug to the receptionist, he was captivated by a fan of autographed photos behind her desk: movie stars wearing Leonardi shirts in their films. Wow, he thought, this is great. Imagine if we could be a supplier to Leonardi and see our shirts in the movies.

Then he felt the butterflies in his stomach. Doubts arose. He suddenly felt insignificant. He wondered if he should even be in such a great place. What gave him the temerity to dream he could do business with such a global enterprise? He really should have called ahead. Had his eagerness betrayed him?

"May I help you?" offered the receptionist.

"Yes, I'd like to see Roger Burdick, please?"

"And your name?"

"Zaine Nasir. I called him from San Francisco the other day."

"I'll tell him you're here. Please have a seat."

Zaine sat in the corner by the waterfall. The receptionist spoke with someone on the phone, then called Zaine to her desk.

"Mr. Nasir, Mr. Burdick will be out shortly."

Zaine's pulse beat faster as he returned to his seat and picked up a magazine.

Soon, Burdick entered from a side hallway.

"Mr. Nasir?"

"Yes," answered Zaine coming to the center of the lobby to meet him.

Roger Burdick was a tall man with a narrow face. His wavy hair lay flat on his scalp. Zaine guessed him to be 35.

"How can I help you?"

"Well, I, that is my father and I, produce shirts in Batupura, that's near Kuala Lumpur in Malaysia, and I wondered what the procedure was for producing shirts for your company. I brought some samples to show—"

"Actually, I'm more in the logistics area. I see that our suppliers get the piece goods and check on delivery times, et cetera."

Zaine remembered his father telling him to stress the quality of their shirts. "Couldn't you just take a look at my samples?"

"Zaine, I'm up to my eyeballs in work. I'm not the one to judge your workmanship. Sorry," said Roger extending his hand to conclude their meeting that had hardly begun. Zaine instinctively shook his hand, Burdick walked away and Zaine couldn't think of a thing to say. He was left standing there, his box half opened, his moment come and gone. He didn't know what to do, and, like a robot, walked to the elevator and pushed the down button.

Lying on the bed in his hotel room, he was upset with himself for not being more assertive, more persistent. "What the hell am I thinking?" he said aloud. "I'm 27 years old, show up without an appointment—in a short sleeved shirt, no less—with a crummy box under my arm. I'd have thrown me out, too. What the heck is the matter with me? I caved. Now how am I going to get back in?"

He had resolved on the flight to New York that he would first try to get more business for his father, then start looking around for something *he* was interested in. But his resolve was slipping. The confidence the Army instilled in him was waning. Did I really expect Michael Leonardi to welcome me with open arms and sign me up as one of his suppliers? And aloud, "What have I accomplished for my father or myself? Nothing."

He rationalized that maybe Rayna was wrong. Maybe finding your passion in life wasn't something that everyone had to find. Maybe a quiet life in the country, like in Batupura, was exactly where he'd be happiest. How did they know what was good for him? But then he realized that, in truth, he really didn't know what was good for him.

He took Rayna's first letter from his suitcase, flopped down on his bed and re-read it.

"*. . . you cannot live—really live—without a passion for your work.*"

The phone rang.

"Hello?"

"Hello, son. How are you doing?"

His heart flip-flopped. "Hi, father. I'm doing okay," he muttered.

"Did you get the shirts and Rayna's letter?"

"Yes. Thank you."

"You don't sound yourself."

"I, uh, I guess it's a little jet lag. I'm fine."

"Have you gone to Leonardi's yet?"

"I'll see them tomorrow," he lied. He didn't want to lie to his father, but what happened today, well, he just couldn't talk about it now.

"Listen, the reason I'm calling, son, I got a call from Mara Hashimi."

"Un-huh."

"You made quite an impression on her and her niece. She called to ask how you were doing. I told her you were in New York, and she got all excited."

"Why?"

"Do you remember her telling you about someone named Curtis?"

"She read his letter to me."

87

"Well, he lives in Morristown, New Jersey. She said he's an executive with a power company. She hoped you could look him up."

Zaine sighed. "I'll try, father."

"Well, I hope you can get together with him."

"What's his last name?"

"Tredway. Curtis Tredway."

"Curtis Tredway," he repeated as he wrote the name on the hotel note pad. The last thing he felt like doing was meeting 'the little boy who didn't know what he wanted to be when he grew up'. Two losers getting together, he thought. Just what I need. He changed the subject. "Any new orders, father?"

"Ah, no. Maybe something next week."

They said their goodbyes, and, out of respect for Mara, he dialed information for the number of the power company.

To his surprise the power company said Curtis didn't work there anymore. In fact, he had retired some four years ago. He again called information for Curtis Tredway in Morristown, New Jersey, got the number and dialed.

"Hello."

Zaine was surprised at the rich bass voice.

"Is this Curtis Tredway?"

"Yes, it is. Who's calling?" asked Curtis.

"I'm a friend of Mara Hashimi. My name is Zaine Nasir. I'm from Malaysia on business in New York. Mara asked me to call you."

"Mara Hashimi," Curtis said stretching the vowels in her name. "My goodness, it's been 40 years at least. How is she?"

"She's fine."

"Where did you say you were?"

"At le Parker-Meridien Hotel."

"Are you staying for a while?"

"Ah, a couple of days I think."

"Do you have any plans for tonight, Zaine?"

"No, not really."

"How about dinner at my house? It'd be great to see a friend of Mara's." Curtis gave Zaine his address and how to get there. "The whole trip should take you about an hour. See you around six?"

"See you then, Mr. Tredway."

Zaine hung up the phone. He didn't look forward to talking with Curtis Tredway or anyone else for that matter. For the first time on his trip, he considered going home.

89

# ELEVEN

IT WAS DUSK WHEN ZAINE STEPPED OUT of the taxi at the home of Curtis Tredway. The house was on a rise with a curved fieldstone walk bordered by low evergreen bushes leading to the front door. An old fashioned coach lantern bathed the entry with a warm, yellow light. Zaine pushed the doorbell button and turned to look at the homes across the street: brick homes, stone homes, substantial homes.

The door opened and a tall man with silver hair beamed a welcome. Beside him, with a ball in her mouth, was a golden retriever wagging her tail.

"Come in, Zaine," he boomed. "It's good to meet a friend of Mara's. This is Edna," nodding to the dog. (Edna appeared to be smiling at him.)

"Hello, Edna," he said patting her head as he entered the parquet foyer. "Thank you, Curtis, for inviting me to come over."

"Come on back," he said taking the ball from the dog and rolling it down the hall. Edna dashed after it and met them in the family room.

Zaine settled on the green and cream sofa. Edna squeezed by the coffee table, sat in front of him and put a paw on his knee with the ball in her mouth, grinning.

"Can I get you something to drink?" asked Curtis heading toward the kitchen. "I'm having some wine. Like some?"

"Yes," said Zaine rubbing Edna's neck while taking in the richness of the room: a fieldstone fireplace with framed family photos on the mantel flanked by two candle lamps; across from him a large entertainment unit and next to it, in the corner, a child's red wagon. Flowers on the fruitwood tables and the warm glow of lamps made the large room cozy.

Curtis returned. "My wife will be down in a little bit," he said handing Zaine a glass of wine. He was dressed casually in a blue button-down oxford shirt, soft chinos, and worn polished loafers.

"Well, how is Mara?" he said in his warm bass voice as he sat in the club chair across from Zaine.

"Very well. One sharp lady."

"Always that," he agreed.

Edna lay down with the ball between her paws looking up at Zaine.

Curtis asked, "How's she doing now?"

"She lives with her niece, Azizah, and wears sneakers with a swoosh on them," he chuckled.

Curtis smiled. "And does she still make that funny sound through her nose?"

"Oh, yes. The *k'hm* sound," Zaine demonstrated.

"That's it exactly," he laughed.

Mrs. Tredway entered the room wearing faded jeans, loafers, and a polo shirt with the lion logo.

"This is my wife Laura."

"Pleased to meet you, Mrs. Tredway."

"So what are you two discussing?" she asked clasping her hands and resting them on the back of her husband's chair.

"Zaine is bringing me up to date on Mara."

"She showed me the Christmas card your husband sent a couple of years ago."

"Really?" said Curtis.

"She loved what you wrote, 'I think of you often with joy and respect'. What did she do that made such a lasting impression?"

Curtis sighed. "Mara was always so—up. Nothing seemed to take away her cheer. She made each day a new adventure." He paused, letting his head rest against the back of the chair, and looked up at the ceiling.

Laura Tredway sat on the sofa with Zaine.

"If I were to choose one incident in retrospect, it would be the time I had scarlet fever and had to stay in bed for a couple of weeks. She read to me. One story was by Hemingway, *The Big Two-Hearted River*. Nick Adams is on a camping trip up in Michigan, and he's traipsing through the woods with a knapsack on his back. He's beginning to sweat through his shirt. He stops by a clump of ferns, cuts off a few leaves and places them between his back and the knapsack. As he continues hiking, the knapsack rubs the leaves releasing their aroma. I told Mara that I didn't know what that smelled like.

"When I got well, she bought me that red wagon over there," he said gesturing to the

94

corner, "and took me for a ride in the woods in back of our house. She stopped by a cluster of ferns, cut off a leaf and handed it to me. 'Rub this between your palms, hard,' she said. 'Smell the aroma? That's what Nick Adams smelled'." He smiled at the memory. "So what did she say about me after all these years?"

"She said your life was planned by your parents, and that—"

"Yes?"

"And that you never really found what you wanted to do in life," he said, sorry to have been so candid. To his surprise, Curtis laughed.

"She's right. I spent most of my life doing what my parents wanted me to do. Now wasn't that dumb?

"Deep down I knew what I wanted to do because of Mara. She took me to plays, musicals, and movies in New York City. We toured the radio networks. Television was just getting started, radio was still big. I saw live shows at ABC, CBS and NBC. I saw how they created sound effects—coconut shells for horse's hoofbeats, clop-clop-clop, on sand, gravel, cement, stuff like that. I loved it so much, I wanted to *live* in that place.

Here I'm rattling on about things you're too young to relate to."

"No, that's all right. I understand," said Zaine.

"At school, I acted in all the plays. I remember bringing home a make-up kit," he laughed. "My parents thought there was something the matter with me, my father particularly. But to me that was a symbol of 'I am an actor'. Grease paint—I loved the smell of it!"

Zaine immediately thought of the woman Mara spoke of. The woman who loved the smell of construction work.

"And your parents didn't encourage you?"

"Oh, they'd compliment me on the plays I was in, but they referred to it as my hobby. They always asked me, 'What do you think you'll do when you get out of school?'"

Zaine gave Curtis a knowing smile.

"I knew they didn't want to hear me say I wanted to be in the theater, so I'd say something vague about being in business. But, Zaine, I really wanted to be in theater. I wish I'd had the guts to just do it. But, what can you do? At that age parents have a strong influence over you."

Laura spoke. "Isn't it interesting, Zaine, how

an opinion of a parent or teacher can turn a person off their path? A child is vulnerable, takes these remarks by adults to heart, and remembers them for the rest of their life." She stood up. "I'm going to get us something to munch on."

They both watched her leave for the kitchen— even Edna looked up.

Zaine asked, "So what are you doing now that you're retired?"

Curtis sat up straight. "Retired! Who told you I was *retired*?" he exclaimed.

"That's, uh, that's what they told me when I called the power company."

"Laura, did you hear that? Company told Zaine I was retired. Retired from them, yes. But *retired*-retired? Heck no! I've got a whole new career. I voice commercials."

"How did that happen?"

"I volunteered to record books for the blind. Library of Congress distributes the cassettes all over the country. I thought it would be fun to read a story and make my voice fit each character."

"Wow! That's neat," said Zaine. "That's something I'd have never thought of."

"Someone from an advertising agency heard

my voice and called me to audition for a radio commercial. As soon as I walked into that studio, Zaine, I felt at home."

"It's only *now* you're doing what you've wanted to do all your life?" asked Zaine incredulously.

"He's a late bloomer," Laura smiled returning with a bowl of chips and dip.

Zaine studied Curtis: his silver hair, the wrinkles around his eyes, and, yes, the age spots appearing on his forehead.

"Do you feel you missed out all these years?"

"Missed out? I'm doing it!" he said emphatically.

"No, I mean that you didn't get to do it for, well, 20 or 30 years."

"Of course. Zaine, it's one thing to recognize what you want to do in life and quite another to have the courage to do it."

"But you're still not an actor, right?"

"Wrong. I'm an actor in the theater of the mind of those who listen to my stories."

Laura, taking a seat on the couch, asked, "Zaine, how did *you* meet Mara?"

"My father sent me to her."

"What prompted that?"

"It all started when Rayna, that's my fiancée,

said I had no passion for my work. Said you can't really live without passion for your work. I told my father, and he sent me to Mara to help me find a career I'd be passionate about. That sounds ridiculous doesn't it? Asking a total stranger, 'What's my passion?'" he said affecting the voice of a whiny three year old.

"Asking isn't ridiculous, it's a sign of maturity," said Laura seriously. "Doesn't everyone sometime in their life wonder what they were put on earth to do?"

Curtis said, "Go on, Zaine, what did she tell you?"

"She told me of others who had found what they wanted to do in life, but she didn't tell me how they found it. The reason I'm back in the States is because she said to find out why in a free society everyone isn't doing what they want to do. Seemed like a good idea at the time."

Laura and Curtis smiled and nodded in agreement at the simplicity of Mara's statement. Curtis continued, "So what have you accomplished so far?"

"Nothing really as far as finding a career for myself. I've been concentrating on something for my father."

Zaine related his idea to manufacture shirts for Leonardi and gloomily reported the failed meeting at Leonardi's this morning. "So," Zaine concluded, "I think now I should take a time-out. Maybe go back home."

Curtis asked, "Why would you go home now? You haven't even started to find what *you* want to do."

Zaine sighed, "I got started a little bit. I met someone in San Francisco who tried to be helpful, but that turned out to be kind of discouraging, too. His name is Roy Hawkins. Ever hear of him?"

Laura said, "He's a pretty big deal. Everybody's heard of Roy Hawkins. How did you meet him?"

Zaine told of how he met Hawkins, and then cut to the chase. "He's working on a method to help people like me who are having trouble finding a career they're suited to. He said the first thing you have to do is *access your past* to find your gift. Then you *act on that gift,* and you'll be led to a career you'll be passionate about. Access and act, he said." Zaine paused a moment. "You know what he said my gift was? Organizing and building." He smiled. "Know anybody who needs a good organizer?"

"How did he come to that conclusion?" asked Curtis.

"He asked me to tell him three episodes in my past where I was involved with something that made me happy. From what I told him he came up with organizing and building. Then he said to *act* on that. That was his two step method. Access and act. Big deal, huh?" he said sarcastically.

Laura let the sarcasm go and said incisively, "I think Hawkins is right. Many times when we look to the past—particularly in our youth—our gifts and passion are shown to us. Like Curtis' was. A child's enthusiasm is not from the intellect but from the heart."

"Frankly, I've put the Hawkins thing on the back burner because I've been so focused on getting a contract from Leonardi to help my father's business. Something inside me says I *have* to ask for his business or my father will be *out* of business." He sighed, "But I screwed that up this morning. That's why I need a time out. Go home, maybe, and sort this all out."

"Quitting?" asked Laura frowning and folding her arms across her chest.

"No, I'm not quitting, re-grouping," he said testily.

"I wonder what Rayna would say if you went

home and told her you were *this* close to discovery but backed out because you needed to *re-group!*"

Zaine bit his lower lip. Laura's directness had become annoying.

"Laura," rumbled Curtis gently and with a hand motion suggested she ease up.

"Zaine, do you want to go home to hold Rayna in your arms or to be held in her arms?"

"Laura!" said Curtis. "What a wicked question."

Zaine was stung by Laura's sharpness. He leaned forward, his jaw set. "I didn't say I *was* going home," he said defensively. "All I know is I can't fail Rayna, and I can't fail my father."

"Nor yourself either," said Laura.

He looked at her while taking a deep breath. "Yes, I understand that," he said evenly. "I'm just . . . well, I need a breather."

Everyone sat quite still. Even Edna had paused from gnawing at her tennis ball.

Laura said, "Would you do something for me?"

Zaine gathered himself. Despite her bluntness, he did feel Laura's sincerity. "Sure," he said.

"Zaine, I want you to close your eyes. Pretend you are married to Rayna. You have your own home and children perhaps. It's morning and you've just finished your breakfast, and now you are going to spend all day doing something you love to do."

Zaine closed his eyes.

"Remember, Zaine, not to think about what others would think of your choice . . . not neighbors, not your father, not even Rayna. You get up from the kitchen table and do what?"

"I can't tell you what I'm doing specifically." He thought, they waited. "I'd like to be involved in something where I have to pull a lot of pieces together to make whatever it is happen. I love that challenge, I guess." He opened his eyes and looked at Laura.

"What you've described is what Hawkins said you're good at. You've been unconsciously doing it ever since you saw those shirts in San Francisco. You've been putting the pieces together. Seeing Leonardi is your challenge."

He didn't answer, just stared at her. It couldn't be that simple. "Mrs. Tredway, it's hard for me to take the Roy Hawkin's method seriously."

"Why?"

"It's too easy. Finding the right career couldn't possibly be as simple as he makes it out to be."

Laura looked at him, grinding her teeth. Finally, she spoke. "What is it with you, young man? You are told how to find your gifts, and you say it's too easy. You are told what your gifts are, and you pooh-pooh them."

He shifted uneasily on the couch, as Laura continued.

"Would you rather the process were difficult? Would that make you feel better? You've been trying to figure out what you are suppose to do in life for how long?"

"Well, I'm 27—"

"What have you come up with?"

He shook his head.

"You've been very fortunate to find two people who can help you help yourself. And what do you do? You—"

Curtis cleared his throat. "I think you've made the point, Laura. Zaine, things in life that look simple have gone through some very complex processes." He paused. "Have you ever seen those fireplaces that ignite with the click of a remote? Easy way to light a fire, huh?"

"Yes."

"Now, if a fireplace salesman tried to sell you

104

one of those would you say, 'Oh, no, that's too simple. I'd rather chop down a tree, saw the boughs into logs, carry them into the house, sweep out the ashes in the fireplace, lay in the logs, stuff paper around them, light a match, hope that smoke from the fire doesn't permeate the house, and finally sit down to enjoy it'." He took a breath and leaning toward Zaine quietly said, "Personally, I'd rather go 'click'. The method Hawkins and Laura have spoken of required a lot of thought to make it simple. Simple, Zaine, so you can go 'click'."

Laura stood up. "Before I go to the kitchen, I just want to say this. Everyone wonders what they're going to do when they grow up, and—rich or poor—the feeling of *emptiness* is the same.

"I'm *not* rich," Zaine muttered.

"And you're not *poor* either," Laura said quickly. "Listen, I watched Curtis work for 30 years at something he really didn't want to do. I don't want this to happen to you. I can't stand to see you quit on yourself. Can't stand to see you miss this moment."

Zaine noticed her eyes were moist, and she trembled slightly.

"If I've hurt your feelings, I didn't mean to. I only want you to experience what you love doing—like Curtis does now—without going through 30 years of drudgery. The contrast between Curtis working for the power company and what he's doing now is so great it makes me want to scream at you to find your passion. Yes, I can understand your wanting to take a breather. You've come far and fast in a short time, but I don't want you to stop. I don't want you ignore the *method* because you think it's too easy. And you know what? I think you've found your career and don't even know it."

She took a tissue from her jeans and dabbed one eye. She gave a little laugh as she regained her composure. "I didn't mean to get so emotional, Zaine. I'm sorry."

She had connected. Zaine was moved by how deeply she felt for him. "What do you mean you think I've found my career and don't even know it?"

Laura smiled and came over to the sofa and sat beside him taking his hand. "Roy Hawkins was right on the money when he said your gift was to organize and build. But his method only contained two steps. Access and act. What he failed to include is that you must *accept* your gift. There are three steps, see? Access, *Accept,* Act."

Zaine repeated the words. "Access, accept, act."

"That's right. And *accepting* your gift is the hardest because we think anyone can do what we do, that it's certainly not a gift. But it *is*, Zaine, accept that. Now let's re-visit the *real* reason you want to see Leonardi. Tell me what you feel."

Zaine thought for a while. "How I feel?" He let out a long breath. "To tell you the truth I felt excited the moment I saw his display in the department store. You should have seen it. Maybe they have them here in New York, they must have them here . . . maybe even bigger. I felt a rush inside me that this man, Leonardi, had such a great thing going for him. I wanted to be part of that. All I could think of was, how to get in to see him, to produce shirts for him, to be a part of that big display—world-wide mind you. My father would never have to worry again."

"Zaine," said Laura beaming at how animated he was as he spoke, "let's leave your father out of this. I think your duty to him has you confused with finding your passion. It has clouded your vision."

Laura's knack of getting him to talk from his heart was a tremendous release for him. "Boy, if I could pull this off," he said.

"Zaine, when you were working for your father, did you like the business or not?"

"I'm not a shirtmaker."

"I didn't ask you that. I asked you if you liked the business."

Zaine didn't respond.

Laura asked, "Have you ever thought of your father's business as a business, or did you always think of it as making shirts?"

"Making shirts."

"I see. Yet, all you've mentioned is increasing the business." Laura left a pause. "Is it possible you're on the right path, but because of your perception of making shirts, you've concluded you're on the wrong path? Maybe looking at it a different way can make a big difference."

Zaine nodded his head slowly. Had he ever given any thought to taking the reins of the business? No. Why? Because he unwittingly was still the child and his father was the parent; therefore, he just followed his father's orders. He never en*visioned* taking charge.

Laura broke his concentration. "Do you believe that's possible, Zaine?"

"Yes," slowly, then quickly, "Very much so."

"Here's the important question, Zaine. Please think before you answer. Do you *accept* that your gift is to organize and build, and it's the business of the business that is your passion?"

Zaine thought.

"Zaine, it could be any business."

Zaine could only smile at her.

"You see, Zaine," said Laura, "you *do* have a purpose, you *are* here for a reason. When you believe in your gift, then it becomes easier to make accurate choices."

"Like my choice to try to see Leonardi?"

"Yes. Now, it may not be him specifically, but you are on the right track. Could turn out to be something even bigger than the great Leonardi. You're an innovator, Zaine. You like to enhance things. But because it comes so easily to you, you think anyone can do it. On the contrary, this is your gift, treasure it. It is uniquely yours."

"Damn!" he said. "This is good."

"A few minutes ago, you were ready to go home to re-group," she smiled. "Now, how do you feel?"

"Excited. How did you come up with this stuff?"

Nodding to Curtis she said, "I've lived it." Then she went off to the kitchen.

Curtis moved in his chair, "Click! Huh, Zaine?"

Zaine laughed. He finally accepted the method. No doubt about it, he thought, this was how to find the career he was meant to have—the whole reason for *living*!

Curtis continued. "See that little red wagon over there?" He nodded to the corner. "Mara gave me that. I keep it in the house to remind me to be true to myself—to stay with what she helped me discover, the passion to express myself through my voice. It's the link between then and now. I think if I had this *method* back then I would have had the confidence and courage to follow the career *I* wanted. Yes, Zaine, the method works. Don't wait 30 years to apply it. Do it now! And with faith you'll find the career you'll be passionate about."

The word "faith" struck a chord with Zaine. He recalled his mother telling him the story of the tiny mustard seed. She held her finger and thumb close together saying, "By planting this much faith, nothing is impossible."

On the bus ride back to his hotel, he peered out the window at the twinkling lights of the New York skyline. He marveled at the skyscrapers and thought of the people who worked in them. He thought of the United Nations building and the diversity of people who worked there. Suddenly, in the reflection of the bus window, he saw a big smile on his face because the answer to how to see Leonardi had just come to him.

## TWELVE

THE ELEVATOR DOOR CLOSED, and Zaine was on his way to the offices of Michael Leonardi—again. He had a one o'clock meeting with Rachel Green, Vice President.

The morning had begun with a visit to the Malaysian Consulate, a brownstone building on the east side flying the Malaysian flag above the entrance. After a brief wait in the lobby, Mr. Mohammed Affendi, consul, received him in his office.

Mr. Affendi gave him a background on the protocol of international agreements. Zaine took notes, asked advice, and, then, how to make contact with someone at Leonardi's.

Mr. Affendi explained that the consul trade section only offers *names* of companies for

Malaysian entrepreneurs. Zaine's heart sank, but he brightened considerably when Mr. Affendi said, "However, I workout with a man at the health club who is employed there. Let me call and see if he can direct you to the right person."

Mohammed coolly called Leonardi's and spoke with his friend. He explained that Zaine was in town for a short while, that the quality of his product was exceptional, and he wanted to be a supplier for Leonardi. He was put on hold. "He's trying to connect me with the person closest to Leonardi to see if she can see you," he said with his hand over the mouthpiece. Then, in a brief conversation with a Ms. Rachel Green, he secured a short visit, it was emphasized, at one o'clock.

From the Embassy he went to Brooks Brothers. There he bought a white oxford button down shirt, gray slacks, and a blue blazer. (Just like Roy Hawkins wore.) He lingered long at the tie table. Should it be a red one? A green? A yellow? Paisley, stripes, designs? The salesman suggested the yellow tie with modest designs, bold yet classic. He waited while the pants were cuffed and the jacket sleeves let out a touch. He was understandably nervous—nervous about meeting, hopefully, Michael Leonardi and nervous the people at Leonardi's would see through his ruse.

Zaine's heart beat faster as the elevator approached the top floor. The doors opened, and he walked confidently to the reception desk.

"May I help you?" she offered.

"I'm here to see Rachel Green."

"Ah, yes. Mr. Nasir?"

"Correct. The Malaysian Consulate set the appointment," he said unable to resist the inference that the meeting had important international implications.

"I'll tell her you're here. Please have a seat," she smiled officiously.

He sat by the waterfall. A week ago he had dipped his hand in the water fountain at his father's home, and now he was looking at a waterfall in the home office of a global enterprise. It felt surreal, but soon, he thought, will come the moment of truth. He turned to watch the people streaming from the elevator and disappearing down the hall. Back from lunch, he thought. They all seemed in such a hurry.

"Mr. Nasir? Ms. Green will see you now," said the receptionist.

He was directed to go down the hall to the last office on the right. As he walked down the narrow corridor, he noticed the double doors at the end.

"Ms. Green?"

"Come in, Mr. Nasir," she said.

Rachel Green was in her fifties, he guessed. She wore a tailored coral suit, accessorized with silver necklace and earings, and on her wrist a watch with large numerals. "What can I do for you?" Her words were clipped, her demeanor direct, but not unfriendly.

He began by telling how he noticed the labels of the shirts in a San Francisco department store and how he thought that maybe—

"Yes, yes," she said impatiently. "Do you have samples with you?"

"Yes, I brought two to show you." Zaine reached for the box he'd brought with him, pulled out the shirts and handed them to Ms. Green.

She leaned forward at her desk to examined them.

Suddenly, a voice on the intercom. "Rachel, would you come into my office?"

"I've someone with me right now, Mr. Leonardi. The Malaysian Consulate sent him

116

over. Be with you in a couple of minutes. We're just wrapping up."

Nothing further from the intercom.

"Zaine. May I call you Zaine?"

"Yes, ma'am."

"How many shirts do you produce a week?"

He was still in awe of having heard Michael Leonardi's voice on the intercom. Everyone seemed to speak so fast and direct, not a wasted word or a wasted second.

"How many?" she repeated.

"A thousand."

"Not enough."

"What do other suppliers produce?" he asked.

"Thousands."

Hearing the double doors open in the next office, Rachel Green stood and gathered Zaine's shirts in anticipation of Leonardi's appearance to relieve her of her guest.

"Zaine, you'll have to excuse me. Mr. Leonardi needs to speak with me. You do good work—it's very good—but come back when your operation can produce 5,000 a week."

Before Zaine could leave, a short man appeared at the door, well into his 60s with a mane of blond hair. Michael Leonardi. The lion of the logo.

"You're from Malaysia?" he said smiling.

Rachel Green introduced them.

"It's a pleasure to meet you, sir," said Zaine.

"Are these your shirts?" he asked taking them from Rachel's outstretched arm.

"Yes. My father and I produce these in Batupura which is a couple of hours north of Kuala Lumpur." He felt he was starting to babble in his excitement so restrained himself.

Leonardi took his time inspecting the shirts.

"How many do you produce a week?" he asked.

Ms. Green interjected, "A thousand."

"A thousand," Leonardi repeated. "Well, that wouldn't do for our regular business, but come in my office. You, too, Rachel."

Leonardi's office was a pictorial autobiography. On the walls were framed photographs grouped by subject: pictures of his family, pictures of the company's early beginnings to present day, and pictures of people in high places wearing shirts bearing the Leonardi logo. Zaine was intrigued because attached to each celebrity photo was a swatch of the fabric the celebrity was wearing.

Comfortable overstuffed chairs and sofas soaked up office sounds making the room feel more like a retreat than a high-powered business office. Leonardi's desk was a large, simple cherry table. His straight back chair had thick arms and was upholstered in a cranberry and cream design. Leonardi sat at his desk, Rachel and Zaine across from him.

"How long have you been making shirts like these?" he asked.

"My father's been at it for, I guess, 30 years. But the factory was opened nine years ago."

"And you produce 1,000 a week?"

"Yes."

Leonardi sat back in his chair. "Did Rachel tell you of our Signature Series?"

She shook her head.

"Well," said Leonardi, "we're introducing a new line next fall called our Signature Series. High quality shirts that will command top dollar. We're presently engaging smaller suppliers whose work is of the caliber of, well, the same as yours," he said fingering the shirts.

Zaine tried to curb his excitement. *Focus, focus, focus*, he said to himself.

"What do you like about our shirts, Mr. Leonardi?"

"Well, one look and it's obvious," he answered. "The single needle, lock stitch, the French bevel pearl buttons . . ."

"We use 22 stitches per button," interjected Zaine.

"And the polished finish. Is this yarn-dyed or piece-dyed?"

"Yarn-dyed."

"Yes. This is the kind of workmanship we like to see. How big is your operation?"

"We produce a thousand shirts . . ."

"No, I mean how many square feet."

"Three thousand square feet. We use the two and ten formula: two cutters for every ten operators per thousand square feet."

"And your machines?" Leonardi fired back.

"High speed single needle. We do have a machine with a computer head—"

Leonardi waved his hand. "Stick with what you have. Those computer head machines are more for home use."

Rachel asked, "How much room do you have to expand?"

Leonardi sat back and watched.

"We have room to double our operation."

"So, you could produce 2,000 shirts a week if you did that," she stated.

"Yes," he answered.

Leonardi leaned forward, "*Would* you double your operation? Do you have the capital to do so?"

"I believe so, yes." Zaine was unsure about committing his father to something without his approval, but he decided to push on. "Are you interested in having us produce shirts for you?" he asked.

Leonardi smiled. "Yes. Based on the work before me, I'm considering you."

Zaine could feel Rachel Green's tenseness in the chair next to him.

"How did you come to see us?" he asked.

Zaine began with Leonardi's impressive display in San Francisco.

"No, I mean how did you get your appointment?"

"I, uh, I needed to see a decision maker," he stammered, nodding in Rachel's direction. "I figured maybe the Consulate could help out. You know, separate me from just someone who popped in with a couple of shirts under his arm."

He offered a boyish grin awaiting their reaction.

Leonardi laughed. Rachel fought a smile.

"So," relieved, "here I am," he beamed.

"Excuse me, Michael," said Rachel, "with all due respect to Mr. Nasir's ingenuity, and not to slight the quality of his shirts, we really don't know anything about his company."

"I know that, Rachel." He smiled at Zaine.

"I can assure you we'd meet your specifications. My father is a stickler for quality. And isn't that your major concern?"

Leonardi continued to smile. Rachel offered no expression.

"What time is it in Malaysia?" asked Leonardi.

"Time?" Looking at his watch, he swiftly calculated the 13 hour difference. "2:30 A.M.," he responded.

"Too late to call your father I suppose?"

"Ah . . . no. We could call him. Sometimes he doesn't sleep too well. Maybe he's up. Shall we call him and see?"

Leonardi chuckled and passed his phone to Zaine.

Rachel Green seemed uncomfortable. While he dialed, she moved from her chair to behind

Leonardi's and spoke to him quietly. Leonardi nodded as she spoke, then looked up at her, smiling, and patted her on the arm. She straightened, took her seat and folded her arms across her chest.

Atan had been asleep, but Zaine spoke to him as though he had not. He told his father where he was, that Leonardi liked the shirts, about the Signature Series, that they were under consideration to be a supplier because of their fine work, and that Leonardi would like to talk with him.

Before Atan could say anything, Zaine passed the phone over to Leonardi. He really wanted to be more chatty with his father, but, based on the behaviors of Rachel Green and Michael Leonardi, he thought he would act as they did, directly.

"Hello, Mr. Nasir. This is Michael Leonardi."

They talked numbers. Soon, Leonardi passed the phone back to him.

All Atan could say to Zaine was, "We'll expand. Well done, son."

"Talk with you soon, father."

Rachel said, "Michael, are you cutting a deal with the Nasir's?"

"Yes, I am," he said with a twinkle in his eye.

Turning to Zaine he said, "You'll receive our specs and return samples in several sizes. Upon approval, we'll offer you an initial run of one thousand dozen. We'll go from there."

Rachel Green seemed relieved that Leonardi could cancel the deal if the samples failed to meet their standards.

"Rachel, while I talk with Zaine, would you mind seeing that Harriet or somebody writes up the agreement? Then come back, please."

It was difficult for Zaine to maintain a business-like face while his insides leapt around giddily.

"Tell me, sir. How did you get started in the business?"

He couldn't have asked a better question. Leonardi loved to tell his story.

"My father was a custom tailor in Verona," he began. "He worked out of the house when I was little, then later moved to his own shop. I learned everything about sewing. I was very quick with the machines. When I was sixteen, he gave me 50 dollars and sent me to America."

"Why?"

"He wanted me to be something more than he was. He felt America was a land where all you

124

had to do was apply yourself and good fortune would be yours. So I came to New York City and looked for a job."

Zaine sat back enjoying the story.

"A kindly man needed an assistant, and I was hired. In my spare time I made neckties. Every time I made a shirt for a gentleman, I sold him a tie."

He smiled at Leonardi's cleverness.

"One day, a very large manufacturer of shirts came into our shop and noticed the ties. 'Who made these?' he asked. My employer told him it was me, and he asked how many I could produce in a week. I told him, and he commissioned me right then and there to make ties for him. He sent us the material, and I made the ties.

"I suggested to my employer that we expand, but he was content with what he had so I decided to go out on my own. Soon that manufacturer was contracting me to make not only ties but also shirts to his specifications. I moved out of the city to a small town in upstate New York. We opened a bigger place to handle all the orders. I started a family, too, and things were very good for us.

"One day my wife suggested I design my own brand of shirts with my own label. It would be a family affair with my sons helping out. And the rest is as you see it now.

"Along the way I realized it was the business that attracted me more than the designing and manufacturing aspect. I love pulling it all together."

Zaine jerked in the chair. Leonardi was using the identical words he had said to Laura.

"Zaine," he said, "there are two kinds of people out there in the world. Those who love to work *in* the business and those who love to work *on* the business. Your father loves to work *in* the business; he loves the feel of cloth, running it through a machine and creating a shirt. You and I, we love the *business* of it all. Some love being the chef, others love owning the restaurant. Right?"

"Mr. Leonardi, when did you *know* it was the business you loved and not the sewing?"

"The moment that man commissioned me to make ties for him, I knew. It wasn't the ties that excited me, it was the business of selling them. I never get tired of pulling everything together— the manufacturers, the buyers, the sellers, the advertisers." He slapped his hand on the table. "That's what gets me up in the morning."

# THIRTEEN

O UT ON THE STREET, Zaine was ready to burst with jubilation. Under his breath he said, "Rayna, I've found my passion. I've found it, I've found it, I've FOUND it! And I'm comin' home!"

He thought, this is what it feels like to love what I do as much as I love Rayna. This is the feeling my father feels when he touches the shirts he has made. This is why those who discover what they want to do find so much joy in life.

Entering his hotel he nearly danced across the lobby floor. He hummed in the elevator, and when he finally closed the door to his room he let out a loud, "Yes!" A charge of electricity ran through him from his incredible success with the biggest shirt seller in the world! He picked up the phone and dialed his father's number.

"Father. It's me. We've got the deal, and I've found what I'm passionate about doing."

"Great! Tell me how it happened. Tell me everything."

"I'll tell you the whole wonderful story when I get home. Oh, Dad, I have a crystal clear vision of how we can build our business world-wide!"

"Well, congratulations, son. I can hardly wait to see you and hear all about it."

"Is Rayna at home?"

"I don't know. She hasn't called."

"Well, if she does call, don't tell her anything. I want to see her face when I give her the news."

Zaine hung up the phone. He couldn't stop grinning, basking in the after glow of his accomplishment. A passage had taken place. The responsibility of the growth of the business had shifted from his father to himself. Their roles had be defined.

It seemed light years ago he was sitting on the veranda of his father's home, feeling like a schoolboy torn up inside by Rayna's letter, enduring the admonition of his father and the anxiety of leaving home. But look what happens, he thought, when you understand what your gift is—when you accept it and act on that gift—and with faith your destiny is assured. He shook his head at the wonder of it all.

His gaze fell on Rayna's note on the night stand. He took it in his hands, stretched out on the bed and read the last line again.

*I think of you often . . . and then I think about you some more.*

He lay the letter over his chest, closed his eyes and smiled.

# FOURTEEN

**H**E WAS ON THE FINAL LEG OF HIS JOURNEY—17 hours of flying time. He read several *Sports Illustrated* magazines, worked the crossword puzzle, and chatted with his seatmate, a young Japanese woman.

Most of the reading lights in the plane were turned off, but Zaine's remained on. He took out some paper and began a letter to the Tredways.

*Dear Laura and Curtis,*

*Thank you for the most significant evening of my life! I'm writing this on my flight home.*

*I have an agreement with Leonardi! Isn't that great? I got my appointment via the Malaysian Consulate. Clever, huh?*

*Leonardi, in the course of our meeting, told me his life story. The upshot was he loves the <u>business</u> of making shirts. Sound familiar? Being led to Leonardi wasn't just duty to my father after all. I was being driven by my passion all the time. Thank you for showing me that.*

*I will stop by Mara's on my way from Kuala Lumpur to Batupura and tell her about our visit. She'll be thrilled, I know.*

*How lucky I am to have met her and been introduced to you both.*

*I'll send you photographs of our factory and of Rayna and me.*

*With warmest regards,*

*Zaine*

Then he took out another sheet of paper.

*Dear Mr. Hawkins,*

*You won't believe my good fortune! I went to New York and made an agreement with Michael Leonardi to produce shirts for him at our factory.*

*But more than that, I met Laura and Curtis*

132

*Tredway—mutual friends of an acquaintance in Malaysia. We discussed your method and what you said my gifts were. Laura said you were right on target.*

*She pointed out to me that the gift to organize and build was exactly what I was doing in trying to contract with Leonardi. It amazes me how that was right under my nose, and I missed it. The reason I was slow to pick up on it was because I hadn't* <u>accepted</u> *my gift.*

*Laura talked to me about loving the business of the business. It could be any business. She pointed out that, based on my past, I loved to bring things together, to complete a project; kind of like a conductor brings an orchestra together to play in perfect harmony.*

*Anyway, you told me to write to you if I uncovered something to add to your method. Well, I'd just add acceptance. The way to find your passion is access, accept, and act.*

*Curtis had a governess who pulled him around in a little red wagon. He still has the wagon, keeps it in his family room as a reminder to always be true to himself. So, I've been thinking. You know those polo shirts with the horse on it, or bear, or, like Leonardi's, the lion? Well, how about a children's line of shirts with a little red wagon logo on it? And with each shirt a tag that encourages the wearer to always follow your heart.*

*Well, Mr. Hawkins, thank you for talking with me. Now I have a vision, and I can put your Success System into practice—all because you gave me a method to help me find the career meant for me.*

*Most sincerely,*

*Zaine Nasir*


And so it was with a clear sense of peace that he lay his head on the pillow and looked out the window into the starry night. Music seemed to swell from the jet engines as he drifted into a reverie of being with the woman he loved— Rayna.

He could picture them together dancing, dancing in the stars. He smiled and the image vanished, the music faded into the rhythm of the engines as the plane soared through the night across the Pacific to the woman with whom he'd share his passion.

# AFTERWORD

$I$T IS INTERESTING TO OBSERVE the experiential skills Zaine drew upon to find his passion.

Zaine took the initiative and willingly met with people he knew he must. By not being afraid to network, his sphere of influence grew. Experts say meeting new people is the most appropriate and effective way to get a job or launch an enterprise.

Zaine's questions to others were most always open-ended; a skill that brought him maximum information.

He was an excellent listener.

Finally, Zaine was willing to try new things. Sometimes it was uncomfortable for him, but he always persisted.

*"How dull it is to pause, to make an end,*
*To rust unburnish'd, not to shine in use! . . .*
*That which we are, we are; One equal temper of*
*heroic hearts,*
*Made weak by time and fate, but strong in will*
*To strive, to seek, to find, and not to yield."*

— Alfred, Lord Tennyson from Ulysses

# ABOUT THE AUTHOR

ARNIE WARREN'S VOICE is familiar across America as a radio and TV spokesperson. His career has taken him from top morning radio personality in Miami to CBS Radio where he was recognized by *Radio and Records* as one of the nation's best interviewers. His voice can be heard on the books he records for the blind for the Library of Congress.

He has conducted seminars from Miami to the Pacific Rim which culminated in his first book, *The Great Connection,* a story that shows you how to connect with others—especially yourself!

Mr. Warren lives in Florida.

*The secret to success is total belief in yourself. If you don't know who you are, how can you believe in you?* THE GREAT CONNECTION helps you understand who you are: your behavior style and the effective and ineffective traits in that style.

THE GREAT CONNECTION is a story of Bob Hathaway in a career crisis. His dictatorial boss demands that he change his style from an affable radio talk-show host to a controversial pit bull. A stranger, Doc Crater, slowly changes Bob's life with profound lessons—lessons that will resonate in your life, too.

You'll discover what holds you back, what launches you forward. You'll understand how to get your prospects, clients and family members talking so you can connect with them. But first you'll learn how to connect with yourself. That's THE GREAT CONNECTION! The companion to FIND YOUR PASSION.

## Delivers its powerful promise.

*"Must reading for anyone seeking to maximize sound business and personal relationships."*

Douglas S. Campbell, Senior V.P. Morgan Stanley, Dean Witter

Over **50,000** Sold

$12.00 plus shipping. Quantity discounts available.

arniewarren@msn.com / www.greatconnection.com